Put a Smile On That Face

Also by Dominic Kirwan and published by Ginninderra Press
Where Words Go When They Die

Dominic Kirwan

Put a Smile On That Face

This book is dedicated to You.

I would like to extend special thanks to Bridget Kirwan
for her tireless, creative help

Put a Smile On That Face
ISBN 978 1 76041 259 3
Copyright © Dominic Kirwan 2016
Cover image: *Put a Smile On That Face* (originally titled *Framed and Hung*), an original work by Dominic Kirwan

First published 2016 by
GINNINDERRA PRESS
PO Box 3461 Port Adelaide 5015 Australia
www.ginninderrapress.com.au

Contents

I	9
This is a Public Disservice Announcement	11
Vampire	18
Serial Killer Blues	20
Advertisement for Axes	22
Invisible Emperor	24
Benevolent Psycho	27
The Last Funeral	29
Happenstance	31
Carjack	32
It's an Emergency	36
The Plagiarised Heart	37
Naked	40
The Internet	45
II	47
Imagine Notion	49
Addict	53
Almost a Dance	55
And then the Rain…	58
Munching on the Crayons of Madness	59
A Shameless Plug for my Sink	62
The Leper	66
Dead Space	69
Side Effects May Vary	70
Archibald	72
Toy	80
Why Do You Wear Black?	82
Enemy	85

III   87

- The Soup   89
- Chicken Little Was Right   94
- Nightclub Anatomy   97
- Jukebox   99
- War Is Something That Happens to Other People   100
- Empty of You   102
- The Lucky Ones Always Leave In Hearses   104
- An Inconvenience   107
- Netherworld   111
- Beautiful   112
- A Headless Body in a Topless Bar   115
- Words   118
- Fading   120

'Poetry is like the truth – most people fucking hate poetry.'
Overheard in a bar by Adam McKay, director of *The Big Short*

I

This is a Public Disservice Announcement

1.

Forget the silence
It has moved on to a quieter place
Forget about the foot on your head
The water is a welcome change
And its depths are worth exploring
Forget about swimming
Get on with drowning
It builds character

Forget all you have remembered
Just so you can experience
That illuminating rash
Spreading on your psyche
When you remember it all over again

2.

Listen to everyone
Believe not a word
Only the fools can be trusted
Only the dead can truly be loved

Perhaps the colour blind
See the world as it truly is?
Maybe only the deaf
Can hear what is actually going on.

We need light
To recognise the darkness
That surrounds us
The blind have no such handicap
Yet they bump into things
That are not there

If you are completely blind
And you are reading this
I can sympathise
Something needs to be done
The light at the end of your tunnel
Does not come in Braille

If you are completely blind
And you are reading this
You really are doing quite well
But you may be a hapless victim
Of gross misdiagnosis

Do you see what I mean?

3.

Peer beneath the surface
Beneath the glory and the waste
Wear your finest rags
Throw away your masks

4.

You can tell a lot about a country
By the physical size of the poor
If you see an obese homeless person
Don't buy them McDonald's
Buy them crack cocaine
It's cheaper than a gym membership
And it works

5.

You know you are fat and old
When you buy all of your clothes from Target
Target shoppers are rarely aware
What is written on their T-shirts
As long as it fits
They no longer care

You know you are fat
When the fat bastard section
No longer caters to your size
Luckily there is a fatter-than-fat
Fat bastard section
In a secret room out the back

If you look sad, confused
And morbidly obese
The staff will give you a key
If nothing fits
There is a fatter-than-fat, fat, really fat,
Fat bastard section
Beyond that
If that doesn't work for you
It's time to buy a Moo-Moo

6.

Self-help books
Were written by somebody other than you
Don't read them
Help yourself
Throw them in the bonfire
Along with your brassière

7.

Travel is over rated
The rest of the world does not care
Whether you visit it or not
The distance between A and B
Is an illusion
It's far quicker
And more expedient
To stay put

8.

All we are
Is an idea
Dreamt by an idiot
All we are not
Is the point

I would now
Like to extend a sincere apology
To God
Sorry
That was a cheap shot

But you did not write the Bible
And nobody in their right mind
Has ever bothered
To read it cover to cover

It's a fascinating book
With no discernible plot
Very little character development
Brimming with violence
Death, damnation
And eternal love
It was written by dinosaurs
The Easter Bunny killed Santa Claus

I am up to page 69
I am not in my right mind

9.

If anyone says:
'Life is a journey, not a destination'
Visit the cemetery
There are smarter people
Six feet under
Bring a shovel
Free as many as you can

10.

If you go with your gut
You need to lose weight

If you go with your instincts
You are just another animal

11.

If you can count your true friends
On one hand
Pull the other one out of your pocket
And start typing

Your new Fakebook account
Will be a social media miracle
And you will never be more popular
Or imaginary

12.

Above all
Remember to wash your hands
When you are done
Germs are quite dangerous
Death is contagious
Yet strangely hip
In certain social circles

Below all
Remember to breathe
We don't need another martyr

13.

Put away your pen
Pick up a sword
If you kill enough writers
You'll get a literary award

And whatever you do
Do not rhyme!

(Not this time)

14.

Oh… Fuck it.

Vampire

I miss kissing your neck in the mornings
I miss the taste of dried blood on punctured skin
I miss the repetition
I miss the repetition

I miss missing you
I miss napalm and moisturising cream and that burning feeling
I miss believing in kind lies and convincing smiles
I miss being too thin and awkwardly handsome
I miss thinking I was better than this
I miss praying and thinking someone was listening
I miss getting lost inside you
I miss love
I miss the repetition
I miss the repetition

I miss genuine laughter and indifferent humour
I miss my childhood and how it warped me
I miss playing in mud and being run over by cars
I miss playing games worth losing
I miss the way you missed me when my mind went missing

I miss lost and found posters with my face on them
I miss finding myself and turning myself in
I miss life and painless wandering
I miss the outside world

I miss the inside of nightclub coffins
I miss meat markets that promised fluorescent death
I miss holding you and feeling your breath in my ear
I miss your tongue in my mouth
I miss reading poems that made me want to write them

I miss the repetition
I miss the repetition

I miss hangovers that made the night before worth it
I miss songs that made me cry for no reason
I miss reality and how it tricked me
I miss my memory and how it reminded me of you
I miss being misunderstood in a good way

I miss knowing why I am writing
I miss writing words that truly belong together
I miss thinking I'm hot shit when I'm faking it
I miss licking your face and tasting salt
I miss passion and exquisite delusions
I miss remembering dreams that made sense
I miss nightmares with happy endings
I miss kind mirrors and the sick clown in me

I miss you
I miss me
I miss everybody but I don't answer their calls
I miss the point of it all

The mist is steadily creeping in
I am devoured by folly and nonsense, madness and regret
I have been conquered by the storm

Still, I will miss tomorrow most of all

Serial Killer Blues

I am a famous Hollywood actor
I am a paparazzi pizza delivery boy
I have killed 37 people
The police are onto me…

And when it's dark
I get busy planning my own funeral
And when the lights come on
I am still dead behind the eyes
I expose myself to strangers
They are generally unimpressed
I do a dance when no one is watching
I wiggle my tush for the cameras
I like to make it rain

I have a secret:

(a) I am an Emosexual
The tears turn me on

(b) I am an Arseist
A navel-gazing sadomasochist

(c) I wear black
But my knickers are pink

(d) I am a martyr
An invisible rock star

(e) I am made of Swiss cheese
My holes are the whole of me

I guess it's no secret any more

In the time it took you to read this
I killed another 68 people
The death toll is rising
The police are closing in…

If you keep reading
You are a partner to this depravity
You are just as guilty as me

I need some place to hide
Man
Just until all the media attention dies down
Man
Just until the meds kick in
Man
Just until my victims rot
Man
Just until the bodies decompose and I can come up with an alibi
Man

There is something lingering behind your eyes
It is making me uncomfortable
I can remove it if you like?

There, that feels much better doesn't it?

It will all be over soon
Don't try to speak
Just let it all go
There's no need to thank me

That's just the kind of guy I am

Advertisement for Axes

1.

The television told me
I am expendable, entertained
By hyper reality circuses
The mass media stole my mirror
Handed me my own head
On a salad platter, garnished
By popular consensus

2.

The television fills my hole
My one grave, mistaken
For a pot hole in the road
On the way to war
The television tells me
Heroes are fighting
On the front lines, dying
So I can be forgiven
The television is selling Jesus
It is saving faces
With the money, rolling in
Like tanks over protesters

3.

Shaking, crying out for someone to listen
I put an axe right through the screen
Of my best friend, the television
He merely laughs, now manifest
He swallows us all, devourer of axes
Spits back our handles like toothpicks
Scattered over fields of tombstone teeth

4.

Still, we build fires, pyres
With the minds he has taken
Our eyes dull, souls blunt
Hypnotised, mirrored in the calculated blaze
Of all that we destroy in his name

Invisible Emperor

Old man in a public housing flat
A gift from a government department
He never voted for
He can't figure out the television
Some bastard hid the remote

Old man does the dishes
Everything else is clean

Old man falls over in the shower
Blood, oozing from the split in his lip,
Trickles down the drain

Old man rises
Slippery bones and brittle muscle
Groaning against the relentless tide
And the downpour of indoor rain

Now standing, he washes away the stain
In a bathroom mirror
That doesn't see him the way it used to

The mirror needs fixing
Everything is broken
But the bastards
Those sons of bitches
They never fix a goddamn thing

He puts on a royal robe
The vestments of an invisible emperor
Claws his way to an open window
And just stares into the open street
Eyes blank and formless
Lips cracked like broken pills
Once mashed by bored nurses
And fed to him in angry porridge

Now a monthly needle
Replaces everything but solitude
No more spoon fed gruel
No more electroshocks
He has forgotten what amnesia means

Now the window sill
Offers him a glimpse of the outside
And a stage for his impotent rage
But there is nothing worth screaming
There are no dreams any more
He pulls the curtains closed
Like wrinkled folds of skin
The outside world disappears completely
Just briefly
Yet it may as well be gone forever

He sits in an arm chair
Stares at an empty screen
Flat
Like they say the world used to be
Waiting for his favourite show

As if the dead television would know
Nothing worth watching
Nothing worth being
Nobody visiting
No family or friends
Just burnt toast and eggs
Like a split mind
Scrambled
By the depredations of time

Benevolent Psycho

All my friends are famous
You won't see them on the tube
Channel surfing with the blinds down
Searching for a better way to be confused

I must be missing something
The Devil's deep in prayer
I must be kissing someone
That isn't really there

All my friends are famous
Red carpet riding
On their souls and under heels
All my dreams are dangerous
I know how famous feels

The benevolent psycho
Impersonating Jesus
To find a darker blues
The belligerent Elvis
Feeding his indifference
Nothing left for him to lose

Grandiose conspiracy
In on the outside
Delusional infamy
Shadowing the bright side

I must be missing something
Falling in and out of bed
I must be kissing someone
I must be out of my head

Solipsistic cancer
Reaching through the bars
Devoured by the martyrs
Swallowed by the stars

The Last Funeral

When the funeral director died
No one quite knew what to do
Thankfully, in a show of stunning foresight
He had left behind a list of instructions
To be followed exactly
In the unlikely event of his passing

Black balloons lifted his coffin into the sky
Mourners shot at it with BB guns
Being somewhat inexperienced with firearms
They missed him
The funeral director's casket soon disappeared completely
Drifting into the ether
A vanishing black speck in the eye of the sky

So at the official wake
Of the official funeral
Of the last official funeral director
An announcement is made:

'There will no longer be any more funerals.'

Death is standing next to a bowl of spiked punch
When he hears this
He adjusts his burning, syphilitic testicles
Shifting them just a little to the left
This sudden, unexpected news
(although it should have been blatantly obvious by now)
Rips through him like wildfire

Death realises
That this truly is The End
He is out of a job
He sighs
He grips both sides of the punchbowl
He dunks his face into the fruity slop
And like a pale horse at a septic watering hole
He proceeds to drink

Three raucous hours of drunken debauchery later
Death is dead
According to the coroner
It was alcohol poisoning
According to those who knew him
Death died of a broken heart

There will be no funeral

Happenstance

These words
They fear themselves
An insolent shudder
A cold embrace
Lame lovers limping into mass graves
Awaiting the steady shovelling
Of cover up dirt

The rocking of my cradle
A grown man crying like a baby
With paper cuts in his eyes
Blood streaming down pallid cheeks
Filling every crevice without release
Just the rapid drying of red
Just the ink
Squirming in permanence
Raging against betrayal
And petty trusts mislaid
In favour of misogyny
And repetitions thrown like ink bombs
Exploding
Against blackened windowpanes

I cannot see outside of this room
I cannot see the faces that mock me
But rest assured
I can hear you shaking
In that dimly lit chamber
Of happenstance
And I know what you have done

Carjack

The Fiend's lip curls back
Revealing a foetid sneer
His neck vein pulses
Absorbing particles of alchemical enmity
From the balmy night air
Flooding his neural pathways
With rivers of mercury
And implacable, melancholic violence

He calmly studies the Creep
Cowering below him
His eyes like bubble wrap, bugging out
Begging to be gorged, popped
His tears welling into a pool of snot and blood
Enveloping the shadows
The Road glistens with moisture
A tarmacadam stage
Beneath the Creep's grazed knees

The Creep prays, swaying
A twitching mantis crying out
For some absent Insect God
To deliver him from torment
To bust open his slackened jaw
Like Heaven's gate
And let the flies out
And all of the remorseless Angels
Waiting in the unbearable eternity
Between staggered breaths
For this torture to be over with
Done

'But I won her…fair 'n' square,'
The Creep gurgles.

The television screen behind his eyes
Contracts into a pin prick of vermilion light.

'Life is unfair,' the Fiend says coldly.

'For everyone but you,' replies the Creep.

The Fiend almost smiles
Almost

The Creature's lights cast their judgement
Cold and unforgiving
Her calculated gaze
Molten, high beam eyes
Hovering over the Road
Watching as the Fiend uncoils

He raises his fist
Blistered skin stretched
Over a throbbing meat club
Raw nerve endings entwine
Exposing bloodied knuckle bones
He brings it down, a gavel
Striking the Creep in the temple
The vicious connect, a dull thud devoid of echo
Breaking like egg yolk
Over a pummelled, falling membrane
Precious life leaking from every orifice
As his body crumbles to the ground

The Creep's tongue lolls from the corner of his mouth
A parched slug licking at the asphalt
The world swirls, fading
His finger nails claw at the Road
Attempting to tear out chunks of black, arcane tar

Wrath, pitched like prophecy
Bathes a sapped, defeated mind
In grease, petroleum and battery acid
In oily moonlight

The Fiend nudges the Creep
With the steel toe of his boot
Just to see if he is alive enough
For more of the same
Yet the body lays inert
Revealing vanquishment
And the sweet nectar of destiny

The Fiend stoops down
He peels back the Creep's clenched fingers
Stubborn, even in death's thrall
He takes it back

The Creep,
The Gambler,
The Cheat,
That scurrilous Thief
He failed to understand this:
She has always,
She will always,
Belong only to Him.

The key turns in the wound
The Creature is sick
She splutters, coughs, hisses,
Throwing a fit
Then suddenly, the veil lifts
The Creature recognises her passenger
And roars…

The Fiend grips the stick shift
He plants his foot, flooring it
Her rubber wheels squeal like stuck pigs
Racing in frenzied revolution

Alone and unfettered by earthly matters
The Fiend drives away

Now there is only the Road
Thousands and thousands of miles
Of unrepentant, maddening, broken white lines
Stretching far beyond the reach
Of mortal men

It's an Emergency

an ambulance lights flashing siren squealing
makes a pit stop at the Chardon's Bottle O

drive through and a man calls through
the open window for immediate assistance

he says they're low on anaesthetic for a
patient and he needs two bottles of vodka

for the guy in the back cos he's lost a lot
of blood and he is in incredible pain so can

he get a six-pack of Coors light a quart of
tequila and a lime as they may not make it

to the hospital in time and maybe some
salt and vinegar crisps and a packet of

Marlboro man is this a tough job the driver
says lighting up a smoke and paying through

the wound down window with some fifties
that he found in the dying man's wallet

the ambulance screams off into oncoming
traffic and the naked Medic tied up and

gagged in the back hopes the madman
with the ruptured liver who bound and

gagged him is going to do the sensible
thing and drive the stolen ambulance

back to the hospital soon as possible as
the crazy fucker doesn't have long to live

The Plagiarised Heart

Lean forward and focus
Try not to shimmer
Scan the cage
The unseen screen
For the bones of words

Penetrate the surface
Break the skin

Ripples waver
Fingers gnarl and knuckles crack
Clawing at your face
Lunging at you
In all of your finery

Let terror be your undoing
Let the puppets in

A verb is a doing word
Every repetition undoes the next
A verb does
I do nothing…but verbs

They reach out to strangle you
To embrace you
To wipe away your weary tears
Gouge at your pretty glass eyes

I want to feel your cheek
Pressed against this page
I want to know your breath
I want to write upon your tongue
So you can taste me, know me

There are dreams waiting here
Without you they will just linger
Yawning, leaning against street lights
Digging graves in treasured traffic islands
And diamond tarmac runways
With bored shovels

You are beside me
You are inside me
The spine of a spectre
Torn from the back panel of the machine
The tendrils of wires
That once held acrobats aloft
Whiz and buzz and crackle
Electricity defines us
Leaves us black and crisp and inert

I have come to rewrite you

This poem is a ribcage
A staircase of spirals
Encasing the white noise
That could only emanate
From the edited version
Of a plagiarised heart

And so I long to unlearn you

This is a reckoning
The last of its kind
Take heed
Awake

We will fill the holes
In our lives
In our paper souls
In our dangling chandelier hearts
With silly putty and icing sugar
With nature's flesh

We will eat life
As if it were a sawdust cake
And it will be sumptuous
And sweet

There is no other way

Naked

Would you look upon me naked?
Would you cover me in shroud?
Would you save your last words for me?
Would they be kind?
Would they be indifferent?
Did I ever make you proud?

Would you hold your temper?
With the palms bending
Burning
Breaking
In your stormy teacup tempest
In the succulent mouth
Of the gnashing maws
Of my madness

Would you render me naked?
Would you tear away my layers?
Would you sacrifice me?
Hold me up just to push me back into the ground?

Would you leave me naked?
Steal my skin and unbuckle my armour?
Would you savour my horror?
Hold my breath in your honour?
Would you allow me to breathe?
On the raging bed of your pale still ocean

Would you clothe me in stages?
Would you read all of my pages?
Would you recognise me?
If I were not so afraid

The silence between us held us together
The truth of our hearts is cruel, malignant
Zealous and passionate
It would be so simple to negate this pain
If only I knew how

I am naked
I am frightened
I am alone

Tear your gaze away
Smother me in sackcloth and ash
Stub out cigarettes in these eyes
So I might hide in the tunnels
Rush through the darkness
Lingering beneath us
Unseen

I cannot look in the mirror
I cannot change what I see

Erase this
It is mindless
Erase this
It is forgotten
Erase everything you know
The pictures of us dancing
In a midlife crisis disco
The imaginary film of us stranded
After love left us
Naked and raped and cowering
Dragging ourselves over shattered porcelain shards
Into the green fire
In the corner of a padded room

Rub me
Into the oily smiles of strangers
Interpret me
In violent glances
In sensual languages
That explain me as inexplicable
That grope for sane meanings
In a universal mind that cannot know us
When we are…
Cold and naked and exposed

I am ashamed of my own soul
Of my plaster cracked heart
My Claymation life
Subsisting on delusion
And fleeting glimpses of a reunion
With ego Lego figurines
From deep inside my shallow, wretched hole

Would you look for me?
If I was hiding
Would you find me?
Hold me close
Smother me in fortitude and saliva?
Would you strangle me?
With your exquisite kisses
Mop up my tears
With your distressed, tangled hair?

Would you take my hand?
Even when it is shaking
Because of you
Would you mistake me?
For someone more lovable
And take me into your home?

A mad
Motionless
Corpse
Twitching for the very life in you
To fuel me
To forgive me
To redeem me
A derangement of letters
This success as a failure
Of a man

Tell me
Could you love me as I am?

The Internet

You are stitched together by self-help blogs and Facebook Memes
You are Frankenstein's monster, his lover, the Fiend
Your skin is a patchwork quilt, ruptured by scars of riddles already solved
Everything you know you learnt from someone else's mirror
If you looked any closer you'd be just another selfie
A button pressed, a flash of vanity captured by the I of discourse
You are a popular culture cog in an unpopularly efficient machine
And your approval rating is exploding in fields of overpriced oil

The fire of your longing is spreading like cheap margarine
Your fame is now a disease easily caught and systematically distributed
Advertisements and mouse clicks are the bait
Rat traps define the minefield you traverse, they deny you
You are not Dorian, you are his portrait
You are not capable of love, you are its cure

I want so much to destroy you that I no longer feel anything real
Yet I am enslaved by your zeal, your opportunity, your mind-fucked
    maps of illusion
I am the numb response to your cavalcade of digital advances

Yes, I am the cancer that is your dance partner
Yet I fear we will win this futile competition
Despite the odds
Together and all alone
In spite of our better selves

II

Imagine Notion

Imagine all the people
Living life in pieces
Imagine in rock icon heaven
John Lennon
Striking crucifixion poses
Puffing out his cheeks
Making bigger-than-Jesus faces
Giving Christ the creeps

Imagine dodging bullets
Always being on the run
Fired like a working class hero
From the chamber
Of a made in murder gun

Imagine all the people
Living life in peas
Drowning in plastic
Microwave safe containers
It's all about twisting the knob
It's all about degrees

Imagine the alien pods
Of pre-packaged
Snap frozen Gods
Commanding the revolving plates
In Satan's baseball stadium
Imagine welcoming the People's Beatle
To sing the international anthem
Imagine the pandemonium
The karaoke funeral

The front-page spread
Imagine the Beatle Dead
All six legs
Twitching in the air
Yoko Oh Noooooooo!
Now all alone
Fighting for peace on the front lines
Of a newspaper
Naked in her bed

Imagine no pigeon
It's easy if you try
John Lennon in an aviary
Angry pigeons in the sky
The bird shit
Their target
With white splotches in his hair
Imagine the beaks of revolution
A new talent show
With an avian Compare

Imagine the box set
A multi-platinum opus
Fading in and out of time
In the Garden of the Octo-puss
As you slip that silver disc
In your jukebox spine
Imagine a Paul
Without a Linda
Imagine a one-legged
Divorce suited Heather

Imagine no obsessions
It's more difficult than you think
No Beatle mania
No purchase incentive albums
No hysteria
Imagine
Not owning Imagine
The vinyl version market shrink

Imagine there's no 7-Eleven
Not even a Slurpee machine
No rancid smell below us
No crusty cardboard custard
No dodgy hot dog steam
No more food poisoning
No use-by-dated mustard
Like it's part of some bad dream

Imagine
There's no Imagine
And all the polls
Are topped by other songs
Imagine Hairway to Steven
And Hotel Can't-Afford-Ya
Competing
For that gong of gangrene gongs

(woo-woo…woo-woowoo…)

You may say I'm not a dreamer
And I'm probably the only one
But that lovely song shits me to tears
Does that make me wrong?

Imagine if the world was actually free
Imagine Sergeant Pepper Spray
Without the LSD
Imagine where all the women fit
In the brotherhood of man
Imagine
John Lennon shot
Right before he wrote that song
I'm not sure that I can

Imagine not imagining
It would really do in your head
Imagine John Lennon
Shot Mark David
After everything's been said

The world would still be at war with itself
Peace still in a darkened hole
Imagine the tempting lure
When Lennon made parole
Imagine the mountains of money to be made
Imagine the inevitable:

The Beatles Reunion Tour

Addict

The surreptitious nature of my station
Is trainless
I left the rails
Many dreams ago
Now all I can taste is asphalt
And hallucinogenic margarine

My hair follicles are cigarettes
Withering into grey ash
Their ends
Are my end
I tap them into ash tray hearts

Insanity
Has withered me
I drink from the fibreglass bosom
Of a mannequin ghost
She sustains me
Puts calcium in my bones
She is imaginary
And so am I
Where to from here?
The psychiatric laxatives have left me empty
My soul dribbles
Like existential mayonnaise
All over this bread made flesh
The wine tastes like blood and destiny
It rushes through my veins
Like perfume and petroleum
Igniting me
Making me stink pretty

Inspiration is a distant companion
I write to occasionally
She never feels the compunction
Nor the need
To get back to me

Is that a sign of entropy on the road ahead?
Or is it just another stop sign?
Should I give way?
Or plough through the red lights
Behind my eyes
Regardless of the oncoming traffic?

Either way
I am a rotting god
Of my own creation

Either way
I am scared of psychoanalytic mirrors
And I'll be damned
But they seem to be everywhere

The egotist needs no introduction
He introduces himself:

'Pleased to meet you…'

Almost a Dance

The moon is shaking
As narrowed eyes hone in
On midnight milk skin
And salubrious, tangled black hair

As she walks towards the water
The tree branches reach down
To caress her limbs
In worship of splendour
Her garments fall to the ground
Uncoiling like silken bandages
And as she falls out of her clothes
Her toes tease the surface
Breaking the lake's watery skin
Ripples of reflective moonlight
Delighting in the tiny waves
Echoing thereafter

Soon her hips disappear
Then her belly
Then the first of her ribs
The bottom rung of a ladder
Encasing her heart
Swathed in succulent nectar
She wades in
And her delicate, willowy hands
Trawl the water in half circles
It is almost a dance
The slowest of descents
The lake cupping her full breasts
The cold lightly stinging her nipples

Then a sudden dive down
A thrust of irredeemable abandon
Leaving nothing behind
But a rash of bubbles
And fragments of weeping moonlight
Swallowed by the gaping jaws of the lake

The minutes pass
And soon become hours
Mutating into an infinite lifetime
Lost
The eyes still watch
Yet there is nothing to see
She is gone

Disfigured, madly muttering children
Climb down from the trees
They fight over her clothes
Tearing at them
Like Jesus' robes
They linger by the water's edge
Nattering like fiendish critters
Gossiping at the chasm she left
Filling it with their stories
Snarling at the water
They are too afraid to enter
Arguing as to why she left them
Here…
On the precipice of reality
Before they could gather the courage
To descend as one
And devour her

The moon is still shaking
The night air has been left behind
For someone else to breathe
And somewhere beneath the surface of the lake
She is smiling

And then the Rain…

And then the rain…
Droplets smattering burnt skin
Scalding hallowed lips
In eternal summers fits
Of humid and human tide swells
Like layers of oily margarine
Clinging warmly
Mingling with the sweat
Like beads of unfathomable leech
Trickling from unshaven hairs
And falling like ill-mannered manna
From claustrophobic heavens
Lingering too low in the sky
To evade the shadows of buildings
That do not tower high enough
To blot out the brown fire

And then the rain…
Descending tangled
And evaporating in rapid bursts
Of moistened gunfire
From the greying Grecian wreathes
Of God's armpit

Munching on the Crayons of Madness

Forget about Orwellian television
I'm First World poor
Huxley was a Brave writer
Yet the Scared New World
Has been digitised
The library burnt to the ground
I danced around the flames
To vintage Van Halen
Like it was 1984

We are being watched
You and I
We are watching ourselves

Thank you social media
I've been seduced by Big Fucker
That sly, adroit Brother
He gave me this canvas
And its edges have no end

Munching on the crayons of madness
Crunching the abs, flab and the numbers
I live, love, cry and die typing
Connected, captivated and bleeding
With a USB flagon of port
The only evidence
Of where my liver used to be

HE makes me feel less alone

Big Fucker plays upon my vanities
My sublime, cyclical insecurities
Now we are ALL published writers
Waiting for the invisible
Reality checks to roll on in
To cover us in abject likeability

IT makes me feel less alone
It's the world's biggest personal diary
Yet how honest are we?
While we know Big Fucker is watching?
Twittering, twattering, following
Narcissistic celebrities
As if that's who we aspire to be

How shallow are these waters?

NEWSPAPER HEADLINE
Elephant Man Drowned in Empty Jacuzzi by the Beautiful People

We revel in watching one another
Staring into streaked, murky mirrors
At the wonder of our projections
At our smitten selfie reflections
Big Fucker sells us things
We didn't even know we wanted
He sells us to ourselves

YOU make me feel less alone

I am not complaining
I 'like' him (clickclickclick)
But my mind, my heart and my body
Are still mine
If that ever changes
I will hand in my resignation
I will pull the plug from the three pronged
Holy Trinity gash in the wall
Open the window to the outside world
Smile…
Then jump

After all
The sun is shining
The birds are burping
It's only a half-metre fall
And I really could do with a walk
In the real world

A Shameless Plug for my Sink

Let me comfort you
Hold your hand
When it is shaking
Let me connect you
To the mainframe
Strap yourself in
For the latest ride
Of your life
Before the next one begins

Cracks in killer shark tanks
Crazed lovers
Raiding blood banks
For that inflected haemoglobin fix
The unholy army
They're wrong on time
Wearing cattle ticks
Like unwatched watches
With bombed out faces
And quivering hands

Our heroes
Our ghosts
Our lovers
They are falling apart

Possessed of smiles so wide
They slit the throats of happy people
With happy faces
With giggling, moody genitals
With electric emoji souls
Trying to keep up with the shyscrapers
With artificial eyebrows
That arch like nemesis
Like predictive oral sex text
Blown like the wind

Love, she sold me a fraudulent
Rhyming dictionary
And I never thought
To give it back

I never thought to tear it into pieces
I never thought it was all broken
I never thought to love myself anyway
I never thought to sink my teeth into your heart
I never thought that mirrors
Would see me this way
I thought
And I never thought to think at all

Now I have all the time in the world
To regret these regrets
That I tossed from a sixth-floor balcony
It feels like only yesterday

I can only guess
That someone went downstairs
Gathered them all up
Brought them back to my door
And left them there
Burning
Waiting for me
To revisit them

To choke on my leash
To gag on the smoke
To burn my feet on parchments
And ads for advertisements
That sold me
So convincingly
To myself

Instead
I read other people's suicide notes
Out loud
To an invisible crowd

I unwork for a living…

And I am bathed in a cruel digital glow…

And I think I'll stay Ugly, in a Beautiful way…

The demented architect
Of a blackened soul
Hipsters swinging from the gallows
To the discordant beat
Of a one wondered hit
Ready to fall
Into a Lewis,
Carolled by the candle light
Shallow whole

Did you ever stop to wonder?

All the poems in the world would be so empty
If they described only you

The Leper

When the Leper's teeth began to fall out
One by one
He knew it was not long
Till his other parts followed
Next went his nose
Then half an ear
Soon he could barely sell or smell himself
And his incessant sniffing
Was now almost inaudible

He whimpered
When his left eye
Suddenly
Popped out of its socket
And…
(Watched closely by his right)
Rolled underneath a pool table

It was snatched up
By a bar room shark
It joined the other balls
As if on cue
Upon the felt and feelingless green

Soon there would be nothing left of him
The Leper mused
And the half-beheld mirrors
Of left behind memories
Confirmed his darkest fears

His arm fell off
Dropping
Into the vegetable section
Of an imaginary supermarket
The Leper shedding everything
Save his own
Impalpable tears

A particularly particular thief
Plucked his eyelashes
With tweezers
And the echoes of precision
Rang out
As each Leper lash
And severed disbelief
Mimicked stolen gold
Slashed away
From the eyelids
Of a zealot
They were resold separately
On eBay
For a modest
But arrogant profit

At Sunday Mass
A crotchety old priest
Snatched up the Leper's penis
When it dropped
From the leg of his pants

He waved it around
Admonishing the horrified faithful
In the midst
Of an ever stiffening trance
Making each divine point
With withered dick description
Dotting the air and all of the eyes
Of the gaping jaws
Of the front row flies
In God's halfway-house prison

The Priest scurried from the pulpit
And was never heard from again
He disappeared suddenly
And so did the Leper
Eventually
Still the good news
It spreads like hellfire
Through the crowded pews
Of humanity
It will be replayed
On all of the worlds stages
A way to celebrate salivation
The passing on
Of the divine baton
From a leper unto oblivion
Into blood and bone
To signify the pathos
Raining down on the parts of us
Forever lost

Dead Space

Fire falls, blanketing minds
Engulfing bridges
Isolating cul de sac endings
Caging the exits
Filling the void with filth and smoke

A dead astronaut
Dangles from a spider's web
In space
An eight-legged fiend
Prods at his corpse
Futility rattles like congealed sherbet
In a vacuum sealed jar
The meal is lifeless
The game is over

Love has been here
You can tell

Side Effects May Vary

I am the oily wind
Beneath deep-fried chicken wings
I am all about forgiveness
Even if you haven't done anything wrong
I forgive you
And you and you and…
Forgive me if I am typing too fast
For you to read this

A lackadaisical approach to poetry
Was discovered by this man – '?'
We cannot show his face on television
He is not a dentist
This is not television

Three random acne breakouts
Attacked one escaping prisoner
He broke out
He is free now
And is believed to be searching for ointment
Or God
For whatever heals the problem
The most cost effective solution

A generic brand
Of God
Or ointment
Should do the trick

Side effects may vary according to mood

He is at large
In a small way
He held up three pharmacies
In three days
With his prescription for a gun
Finally fulfilled
He then used the weapon to demand ointment
All of it

The staff laughed
Suggested he needed a prescription
For ammunition
That he should see his doctor as soon as possible
Then come back and try again

Police have urged the public to pray for him

Archibald

1.

In the small hours
Before the scars wept
Before the pharmaceutical angels
Could gobble all the pills
Archibald stabbed at his happy place
With an unforgiving knife
The blade
Reflecting shards of cancerous moonlight
In vermilion eyes

All about him
The world drained of colour
Archibald's gaping vein
Grinned like a leprous sphincter
Pissing nuclear legions
Haphazard mushrooms ballooning
Like opiate bulbs
Like warm Judeo-Christian jizz
Gathering in the small
Of Godot's waiting back

Archibald lied about the way
The mirror saw him
And got away with it
As dots of dark red ink
Sprayed the glass and then fell
Trickling like wanton yoke
From Jackson Pollock bullet holes

Pleased to be eviscerated
Archibald was erect, direct and alien dialect
A stillborn insect
Burrowing beneath the milk white skin
Of finally fucked
Psychotic reality surgeons

He searched for the heart
In humanity
But came up empty headed
His worst memories
Bleating and beating
Like two-legged meat sheep
As they drifted off
Into a vegetative state
Only to be pre-packaged and snap frozen
Finally ready to be devoured
By undead deviants
Threatening bloom and blossom
From the bottom
Of a predator's shit list

Archibald chopped off his own head
With a cheap eBay guillotine
And tucked it under his arm
It was messy, but necessary
A statement of intent
From an imaginative, maladjusted man
Yearning for a literal way
To lose his mind

Nestled beneath his coat
Archibald's head smiled back up at him
Winking that knowing wink
Thank you, it seemed to say
Happy to be finally set free
It saw…everything
It said…nothing

Archibald wrestled with the door handle
That led onto the street outside
With five, red nectar digits
Clawing at freedom
From a slippery gripped, shaking ham fist

His decapitated head
Sipped whiskey from a soda pop can
In the darkness, nestled against his ribcage
As Archibald walked, stumbling, determined
The straw and all it bore
Sent a staccato shot of spirits
Into an eagerly gulping gob
Archibald's soothed, burning throat
Welcomed a river of alcohol
That passed far too easily onto the footpath
At his feet

By now his head was so drunk
It did not care any more
It did not miss Archibald's shoulders
Nor his bloated torso
His scarred, slit wrists
Or his quivering, Aeroplane Jelly legs
It was free to bleed
And to dribble, drool and gobble
Cheap, one hundred percent proof piss
From an imaginary can-can

In its place under his arm
Archibald's head danced motionless
And spectacularly
As if nobody was watching…

(And they weren't…)

As he staggered onwards
His thoughts returned to his troubled childhood
He fondly reminisced
Recalling what his dear mother used to say
Right before she spanked him:

'Archibald, don't lose your head!'

If only she could see me now, he thought.

2.

By the time Archibald reached the park
The entertainment was nearing an end
A woman juggling chainsaws
Lay bleeding on the grass
Nobody called an ambulance
It was all part of the show

A mute mime artist
Did what he was born to do

A monkey beating a grinding organ
Let go of his master's knob
And ran off with a discarded, but still buzzing chainsaw
Screams could be heard in the distance
As the monkey made its way
Through a tightly gathered
Greenpeace crowd
Protesting global yawning

The monkey shaved a chunk of blubber
Off a beached whale
That was marooned too far from the shore
To be convincing
There were no harpoons in sight
There was no way to Free Willy
No inviting ocean
To shove him back into

The Greenpeace protesters wept
And their limbs flew like nightingales
At the mercy of the Monkey's chainsaw toy
Into the salty, blowhole sky

When the hysteria reached its climax
So did Archibald
The headless wanderer
That 'neck-pissing-like-a-fountain' warrior
This was his chance
For Archibald
This would change everything

With regal charm
And the poise of a natural performer
He removed his own head from beneath his coat
The half-empty can of whisky
Scuttled across the lawn

Archibald placed his own severed head
Back on top of his shoulders
And he blinked his eyes
And he batted his eye lashes
As the swirling world
Slowly came back into view

People gasped and flapped
Like fish out of laughter
And immediately
Archibald felt more like his old self
The one that almost got away

'Line up!'
'Line up!'
His head crowed to the gathering crowd
As his precariously perched neck
Wept indiscriminately all over his coat
'It's only blood…'
He grinned triumphantly
'Who wants to go first?'

3.

By the time the ambulance arrived
It was too late
The monkey was dead
The chainsaw
Seeing the error of its ways
Had turned on him

Greenpeace were in tatters
They all vowed to sign a petition
To save themselves

The man without a head
Archibald, the former star of his own show
Mindlessly and blindly
Chased after a group of hooligans
In the distance
Throughout the park
They gleefully kicked Archibald's ragged noggin
Hooting and then booting it to each other
Like a sweating, bloody soccer ball
Across the green, patchy grass

Every now and then
A point would be scored
Something to brag about later
To their mates
Long after Archibald's limp, headless carcass
Hit the ground
And finally ceased twitching

Oh the glory!
Archibald's distressed, bullied head
Struck over and over
By those golden boots
Whistling like zombified missiles
Between the ever shifting goal posts
Of an unguarded, unapologetic
Football free-for-all…

The field of eternal joy

(Insert ORGASM here…)

Toy

Death glances irritably at her watch
Pass the time to the left
She says
Grab a chair when the music stops
She says

I just want to see her smile
So I chase away the flies
I roll in the squalor
Hold her gown above the mud

What are you looking at?
She rolls her eyes
Across the ground
I look down at my feet
And she is everywhere
And everything

Pills in clenched fists
Open
Swaying palms
Scatter white powder
Over black stumps

What so ever shall I do with you?
She throws her head back
She laughs
All mock cross
And driven nails

She smiles
All barbed wire and overbite
She lifts me up by the short hairs
She places me back in the box
Snaps the lid shut

It is suddenly dark
The air retreats
I count down the seconds

Death stands on one leg
And touches up her make-up
All unshaken foundation
Sky liner, lashes and stern lippy

There is no way out
She says
Don't fucking move!

I know
I know
I say
Okay

I hold my breath
I try not to shake

I guess
I am just glad I made her smile

Why Do You Wear Black?

Because it's the colour of your skirt
A wonderful shade of dirt
The beautiful nightmare
I'd rather not forget
Because it's slimming
When I'm swimming
In your smile
It's the new white
The distracted Aphrodite
The peculiar chime
At the end of every dial

Why do you wear black?

So I'm dressed for my own funeral
So you can't see me fading
In the dark
So you won't discard me
When I'm predictable
Explain me
When the truth is indescribable
So I can disappear
When every other colour
Has left a clearer mark

Why do you wear black?

Because it absorbs
The light in your eyes
Because red leaves me bleeding
Green saps my style
Yellow is blinding
Purple is in denial
Because no other colour
Will hide my waist
No other palette
Will paint my faith

Why do you wear black?

So I can make friends with shadows
So I can wade through the shallows
Because I'm too vain to wither
Too sane to consider
Changing places
With the monster in the mirror

Why do you wear black?

Because I'm more sloth than Goth
More solipsistic
Than smoking pun athletic
Because I can't abide
Formaldehyde
And there's no other way to nap
Because it's slightly brighter
On the inside
And I can't buy my marbles back

Why do you wear black?

Because it complements
Coffin nail ash
Because so did Johnny Cash
Because I can't escape the gallows
And I'm allergic
To most rainbows
Because my tailor died
My brain is fried
And in almost anything else
I look like bloody crap

Enemy

Project your ego
Mould your God

There was never going to be a happy ending

Reject your saviour
Smash your mirror
There is no key to your cage
It is not lost
It is not hiding
It does not exist

There was never going to be a way out

Who is laughing at you now?
You cannot see their faces
You cannot know their names
All you can do is listen
Grow small
Shake
And wait…

There was never meant to be a reason

Project your faith
Build your God
Turn yourself
Inside out
You have run out of cheeks
The past
The present
The future

Feel it
As it creeps

Project your guilt
Serve your God
He is a slave to your reflection
The only one to care
He is the selfless condescension
He lives behind your stare
He is the soul in your pocket
He is your finest creation

There was never meant to be salvation

There is nothing you can do
There is only you
The enemy

III

The Soup

I snip away the corner of the packet
With a single pair of non-biodegradable scissors
I pour the suspiciously brown ooze
Containing not one
But hopefully two tiny morsels
Of artificial free-range chicken
Into a microwave safe bowl
That could pass as an ash tray
In any other circumstance

The soup is 99 per cent fat-free
Or so it says
I am one per cent fat-free
Is that why I keep eating this shit?
Do I want to be like the soup?
You are what you eat?
In my experience
And according to my limited knowledge of such matters
You just are
Or you just aren't
Yet I suspect
That I am somewhere in between
An audience of one
A consumer of cutting-edge microwave theatre

I consider reading the ingredients
But it would ruin the mystique
I already know
I will be consuming several artificial additives
Preservatives and sweeteners

I already know
That each one is a number
Somewhere between zero and one thousand
I would Google them all individually
But like I said
It would ruin the mystique
And even if the soup does eventually kill me
I don't want to know how it did it

I smoke a cigarette
And wonder about homicidal soup
About how I should probably quit the stuff
But it's just so convenient
It completes me
Inhale
Exhale
Inhale
Mmmmmm… Soup

Maybe in the future
The machine will tell me to go fuck myself
But it's not the future
At least not yet
It's now
And in the next three minutes
Now will explain itself to me
The secrets of the universe will finally be revealed
Over and over, around and around

I press the Start button
Three minutes isn't a long time
'I am the soup'
If I just keep saying it, it will happen
'I am the soup'
One per cent fat
99 per cent artificial additives
The ultimate me

As the glass plate revolves
The seconds, like layers of unreality
Steadily peel away
Everything that is interesting about the world
Turns like a radiating carousel
Inside the machine

About halfway through the countdown
Of the soup's official launch
The one minute and thirty-four second mark
I realise I just want it to be over with
I am not enjoying the show
All I can think is
I wish the microwave had a fast forward button
And it shames me to realise this
All I know is
If it was microwavable popcorn
Things would be a different

I wonder,
If I could fast forward life through the boring bits
Would I do it?
Am I supposed to savour every moment as if it was my last?

The waiting
The endless queues
The fast food drive-throughs
The advertisements
The pre-programmed programming
The days when you're broke
The time it takes for the medication to kick in
The hours that you can't sleep and there is nothing to dream
The silent pauses
The loud noises
The breaks between coffin nails
The consumption of cheap wine
The point from A to B to Z
On the way to getting so drunk
That you can't even taste it any more
The procrastination
The waning inspiration
Staring at a blank page for hours
Through the window of a computer
That reveals nothing of the world

The minutes put on hold
On the phone
On the toilet
On the escalator
In the lift

In the car park
In the endless pages
Of perfumed, double-ply instructions
That tell you how to use shit
That explain shit
That define shit
That help you get the most out of shit
So that shit will be better

Maybe I should get out in nature more?
Maybe I should go for a walk?
Maybe I should pray to God for forgiveness for being so shallow?
Maybe I should have sex?
Maybe I should do all of the above?

Go for a walk in the enchanted forest of love and have shallow sex with god in a forgiving microwave

'I am the soup'
I just keep saying it
Waiting for the gong
The final beep, beep, beep
That tells me everything is going to be okay

'I am the soup'
I study the revolving stage
The machine says five seconds to go
It is then that I realise something
I am not even hungry

I was just trying to kill some time

Chicken Little Was Right

The days bleed into nights
The seasons into shame
A rivulet of ink, solemn, singular
Trickles like a tear from the corner
Of Time's hand struck face

These numb handshakes
Mask the true shaking
On the inside
They murder the crow collective
Shadowing an internal shudder
That could shrug the very world
From Atlas's shoulders

The sky is falling, insolent
Like a plastic storm cloud
In the hands of a child
Born of madness, the destructor
Descending upon us
His tiny fists beating upon minds
Like blackened hearts, bruised
Rattling the stages, the cages
Of wasted lives spent
In unrealities prism

We feed your wells
We fatten your tears
We make it just
That you should cry
Into the sour milk, spilt
Oozing from the desolate tit
Of the gods you worship

Just so you might suckle, drunk
On life's barbarous jizz

We complete you
We soften the irrational blow
Of your gavels
We who know nothing
We out-wait your miseries
We outlast you
Fill your cerebral corridors
Your sanitised hospitals
With medicated, unwanted filth

The prisons of your multiverse
Contain us
So that you might smile and wave
Safely
At the family car leaving your garage
At the faces of your children
Pressed against glass, soon shattered
By circular revolutions
At your wives and husbands, gratified
By rotting paper slip unions

We who know nothing
Build the paper walls, written
In ignorant fictions, brick upon brick
To protect your imaginary cities
Yet all you ever do is burn us down

We, the fallen
We, the crawling
We, the mind fountain exploding
We are the arbiters of imagination
The taste of us lingers
Like mad shadows in murderous mouths
It can never be washed away

Chicken Little was right
The sky is falling, and soon
Ripped from the ether, tamed and torn
Like a lasso around the moon

Nightclub Anatomy

Her eyes are ovaries
And she stares at me
As though every imperfection
Were a personal affront
To her sense of righteous innocence

She shakes her head
And lion tamers lash
At her perpetually turning cheeks
With fallopian tubes
Wielded like whips
In a spotlit circus cage

Unfertilised eggs
Chug above the alien hordes
On an Atari breast cancer screen
The gunner moves
From extreme left to far night
Spitting pixel missiles
Into a cervical stream

A million sperm bankers
Count down the digits
As they flee from her nightclub womb
Scattering into the violent streets
Outside
In search of another seedy uterus
An all-night bra
That might let them back in

Each is merely a thought
Unthought
Every one
Wishes she would have danced
Only with him
But they were turned away
Semen set adrift on a stormy sea
Disappointed
Drowning
Free?

Love has no place here
It's all about the price of the drinks
Love has no place here
It's all about the music

I held her tightly
And immediately regretted
Everything I had never done

I couldn't understand a word
The sound of the universe was too loud
I yearned to kiss her lips
But ended up failing to read them
Instead

I am certain there is someone else
That I will never meet
Out there
For me

Jukebox

I am the broken jukebox
Sitting in the corner
On the beer-stained carpet
Of a round room
All my songs play backwards
All my loony tunes
Are out of tune
Drunken couples will not dance
To me
Nobody hums along
For long
Pool sharks kick me
For interrupting their games
But they cannot shut me up
Nor can they stop me
I am unfixable

War Is Something That Happens to Other People

Their eyes are bullets
Tearing holes in the fabric of space
Rushing through the chest cages
Of tomorrows soldiers
On the front lines
On dying room chairs
In front of television sets
And hollowed out
Computer fat screens

Their mucus, trailing us
Trickling from the touchable dials
Of destitute prostitutes
And internet whores
Looking to fuck minds
For money
And power
As gun barrels flower
With the evidence
Of their cruel, callous slaughter

Me, I can only laugh
My trigger finger, it taps merrily
On the fire button
And those I kill
I do to amuse myself
Their blood
Spilling like computer-generated jizz
Into the animated pavement cracks
At my feet

Another end-of-level-boss
Goes the way of Jesus
Suffering a violent yet playful death
Only to respawn
Resurrected and willing to die
For my sins
All over again

Every imaginary foe
Each army I crush
When they are gone
They have no families
To miss or mourn them

My victims have no heartbeat
They feel no pain
Yet nonetheless
In all this vaudevillian, paltry glory
I am a murderer, still.

Empty of You

Remove the poker from the fire
Cauterise the walls of the wound
Rip my mind my skin my heart my cold lame hands
From your naked limbs
Leave me mute and alone
Leave me bloodied and singed
Leave me

I only ever meant
What I could be to you
I was incomplete
A court jester with a limp
A black hole filled to the brim
With memories of your pyre

The riddle
The conundrum
I called your name and it was silence that broke me
A fickle and cold facade
Your social front wasted on darker souls

I saw you through the smoke
And I saw nothing
I saw you through drunken eyes
And I saw nothing
I saw you in the netherworld
And still I saw nothing
Yet you saw me
And you cut me
Right in two

We kissed like headless rag dolls
And I knew you were already gone
Somehow I knew
It was the last I'd see of you
I barricaded the door to your truth
And the room disappeared

I listened to your heart
Beating upon the tin roof like rotten fruit
You fell away from me
You sank in your bitter wine

I will leave you to swim happily
Amongst the sweet conceited truth of your judgements
And I will banish you from my heart

I will cry until I am empty of you
Then I will cry no more

The Lucky Ones Always Leave In Hearses

Death is beautiful
At least the living think so
Funerals are attended by the envious
They are driven from their homes
By reality television promises
And persistent telemarketers
To attend the official end
Of someone who would have felt loved
Appreciated
Forgiven
At their own funeral
If only they were alive to witness it

The lucky ones always leave in hearses
The more scrupulous
Scour the thinning pews
Occupied by distraught family members
And temporary mourners and their plus one's
Eager to collect authentic tears
To fill their own eyes
Dry from years of drought

Tongues probe eye sockets
And slaver hungrily over moistened cheeks
Small crystal vials are filled with stolen woe
Then deposited into tear banks
Yet the interest rate is waning
And the tellers dare not cry

An old woman
With a face like a pale prune
Lunges at the lifeless body of her dead husband
On display in an open coffin
She begins to hump away her pain
Thrashing against his corpse like a gasping
Widowed fish
Before too long
Two undercover necrophiliacs
Drag her away

She screams,
'Where's MY orgasm?'
'You son-of-a-bitch!'

Alive
He was a selfish lover
Dead
He is a humpable saint

An altar boy tries to stifle his laughter

A universe of rambling eulogies
Scurry to rewrite themselves

Someone else's God is pleased
As spiked punch

A million drunk photocopy machines
Retaliate
Refusing to break down
They grind out that same image
That same emotion
That same feeling of loss
That same look of fear
All over the world
Copies of copies of copies
Are vomited onto conveyor belts
Transferring unmendable hearts
And broken minds
Unto the garbage dump of oblivion

In the morning all is forgotten
Blackout

Yet the evidence remains
Towering above the emptiness
That defines us
And it is stacked so high now
It could almost blot out the sun

An Inconvenience

She rolls a cigarette
Like she is administering a rubber
To a rigid, syphilitic cock
She lights up outside of the club
That never lets her in
As the first wave of smoke rushes into her lungs
She itches at her stocking and plays with a ladder
As if each step were a rung worth skipping
She needs one more twenty for a hit
The marks on her arms are open
Mouths gaping wide like tormented babies
Toothless, crying for mother's milk

A green car pulls up
The driver waves her over
She wobbles closer on scuffed, red high heels
Stoops down and blows smoke into the blurry cockpit
Of what may as well be an airplane
Her vision is not what it used to be

He studies her face like it is a forgery
Of a Dorian Gray Renoir
They both agree this is going to happen
It will be dirty, quick and profound
In a nothing matters kind of way

She opens the door and gets in the passenger seat
He accelerates onto the road
Like a chariot charging
Onto a winding, tar pit tongue

She continues to imagine a needle
Sliding gently into her arm
Fluid puncturing her vein
Unleashed into rivers of melancholy, bruised blood

The release
And what she needs to do to get there
Are steadily careening towards each other
Like unstoppable forces
Forced to wait
Forever
As if forever was only a matter of time

When the car engine stops
They are overlooking the city
It was a pleasant drive
Her eyes reflect distant street lights
Her eye liner absorbs any uneasy feelings
That might get in the way of the act
That will set her cravings free

He pulls out a knife
The blade too reflects the distant city glow
There is a glimmer of madness shining
As the monster in his eyes takes over
'I'm going to cut you,' he hoarsely whispers
Panting in anticipation
Like a sadistic, hungry dog

He watches bemused
As she wrestles with the door handle
But it is to no avail
She scrambles through her bag
Looking for a can of mace
But it is too late

The knife severs her jugular vein and throat
All the colour happily retreats
Her eyes are no longer mirrors
They are black and white newspaper headlines
Rolling into the back of her head
Like peeled pulps of rotten, pitched fruit
Thrown at the contents of her own brain
From the outside looking in

As the dark blood oozes down her breast and coat
Trickling from the corners of her pursed lips
She somehow knows she won't get that last hit
She is dismayed momentarily
As if this is an annoying setback
An inconvenience
Then she just accepts that she can no longer breathe
That her heartbeat is fading
That she will be dead soon
That she never will get to say goodbye to her estranged family
Who don't give a fuck about her
That God is about to take her
And he probably doesn't like her much either

Hunched over her
Face and jaw splattered with red goob
He licks his lips and squeezes her wet breast
He remembers what his mother used to say:

Finish your dinner or your father will cut you.

He slurps hungrily at the fountain flowing
His tongue lingering and darting
Between folds of severed skin
He thinks of how proud his father would be
For finishing his dinner
That if only he could see him now
Wallowing in the glue
That binds hunger, violence and desire
Drowning in the recesses
Of somebody else's conception of madness

And garbled, misunderstood love
Like a rogue poem shot from the sky
Carries them both down
Beneath the hallowed ground
Far away
From here…

Netherworld

And then I saw you, resplendent, melting in twilight,
of candle light and wax, shape shifter, daydreamer,
a version of yourself, worth being for now,
the map of your mind folding over murky waters,
pontificating, fussing over unfinished tragedy.

And then I saw you, nails buried deep, wings outstretched,
of punctured profanity, thirst and dew drops,
a vision of yourself, blinded by cruel mirrors,
the marble altar, the pill popper, the shit stirrer,
mocking your way to a paradise found.

And then I saw you, the gilded lily, of gramophone mouth,
lucid dreamer and sweetest nightmare, slum lady,
a violence of solitude, jack knifing all prayers,
rogue programmer of personality channels, the beast
chasing tornadoes away, vexing those that love you.

And then you disappeared, same difference, exacting,
the rivers gummed up, damning you, in leaving,
a silence that shook, a jackhammer absence,
where do the words go, I should know, the devil
swept away by the tide, the ruin, the ashen after taste of you.

Of sculpture: this strangeness, the malingering.
Of cracked creation: to never be, to never know.

The netherworld is no longer listening.

Beautiful

Suited vultures without pulses
Circling overhead
The reason for dying
Drinking
Crying
The nip and suck vampire
Vomiting in your head

Beautiful:

The Hollywood leech
Writing that all-impotent Oscar speech
That they'll never get to give
The wolf inside
Every well-meaning sheep
The shape-changing
Fashion freak
The reality hiatus taken
By self-loathing lovers
Of Soya bacon

Beautiful:

The tanned and conspicuous
The muscle toned and malicious
The devourers
Of S&M
And M&Ms
And candy-coated heroin pills
Taken from tenth-storey windowsills

Right before it's time for them to jump
Finally
To the concrete sidewalk
Below

Beautiful:

The lonely, shaking god
In the corner of your eye
The collagen collective
Doing cartwheels in the sky
The angel in the angle
You take to prove a point
The sex appeal suppository
You insert
So you can smile
As you feel it all slipping away

Beautiful:

Game-show teeth
Real fur and fake tits
Miracle white toothpaste
Invisibility cream for zits
The nervous seconds before take off
And the explosion in the air
The miracle of childbirth
The abortion
The despair

Beautiful:

Incomparable anguish
Inconsolable fear
A billion style guides
Burning
In a bonfire of brassieres
The door to dementia
Opening shut
Celebrity face lifts
Decomposing in smut

Beautiful:

The Elephant Man
Grinning
At the head of the parade
The Fat Lady singing softly
Signalling the end
The sickest and most useless
Steering an unsinkable ship
The spectacularly ugly
Out gunning the terminally hip
Discovering a cure
For social cancer
Being an original mover
But a terrible dancer

Beautiful:

Being a joke…
To people who don't usually laugh

A Headless Body in a Topless Bar

When the bell cracked
Like a golden yoked egg
I was poll tolling
I answered their questions
I signed away my last secret
Yet the bullets kept whistling
It was a tune I had heard somewhere before
But could not quite place

On a stage stammering
The shotgun shells danced
Spewing pink powder
Over the front rows
I was all but ready to blitz
So I lucky dipped my organs
Brought a bashful piano
Played an end time tune
As if they were listening

And the Angels fell like tar drops
From the great lung in the sky

When the tarpaulin caved in
I was in on the outside
I watched the clowns flee
Like candy-coated terrorists
I set traps for trapeze artists
The entire circus
Now homeless
Wandered the unlucky lands
Surrounding us

There was a flawed flow
To my afterglow
And I wielded my whip
Like a lame fighter
In a blameless brawl

And the Angels
They fell like punch drunk insects
Into the poisoned palm of my hand
I watched them there
Writhing in the death throes
Crying
Still, I felt nothing

Then again
I may be kidding
I can no longer tell

For my tears are pills
And my heart is a pale inflection
A substitute for a diseased shadow
Flickering like the wings of a suicidal moth
Soon to be aflame
Now there is nothing left but charred abdomen
And the rancid belch of cruel taunting
Echoing in my ears
All else has been devoured

There are no Angels left
Just flimsy, cardboard cut-out souls
Stained by the milk, blood and spunk
Oozing from the damned
Starlit tit
Of a caged killer

Words

I am filled with tiny little monsters
They trickle from my eyes, my ears, nose and arse
I am no more than a vessel, a flesh cage
A squirming meal for sleeping cannibals
With busily pumping veins
Rattling with the chattering of arcane traffic

I am filled with cemetery stones and plastic flowers
I travel from mind to mind
I jump from dream to dream
I am above you, above all
Leaping across the rooftops in the sub-blurbs
I am Satan
I am Santa
I am everyone and no one
There is no time for punctuality
I haunt the corridors of love like a drooling, mangy jackal

I leer at startled spectres, eyeing them with suspicion
As they linger outside the cells of solitarily confined madmen
With no one to talk to but the pretty voices in their heads
With no one to confide in but a motion of no confidence

There is nothing here for me
Just fingernail scars in yawning walls, reverberating
Musical shadows thrown at an auto-tune moon
Endlessly taunting me in a damned tempo
Serenading me with nervous, shaking tambourines and
    trumpet bullets
Like I'm some kind of channel that needs changing
Like I'm in an open casket and everyone is pissing themselves
with laughter

I am a dubious alibi for someone else's crime
I am a rabid, frightened bird, trapped
Smashing and flapping against the walls
As gavels batter bullet proof windows, locked from the outside
Cracks spread like spider's webs, like feigned smiles drying in plaster
Freedom teases me like a slack jawed bully
Parading his thick sculled barbs before an army of devoted cowards
Cornered now, fallen, cowering
As bloody feathers rain from the concrete sky
There is no way out
There is nowhere safe to rest my eyes

Words are violent
Words can kill
Words can save your life
Words are all that I have

Fading

How I fade away
Into this shadow
Of an older man
How the stars too fade
How the gutter
Becomes both comfort and casket
The marbles lost
The clink of yesterday's glasses
Lending a bloated guile
To fangs fixed
To a crazed boy's throat
A boy I can barely remember
Any more

The lovers lost
The smell of dried kisses
Like brown leaves
And leavings, clenched
In withered fists
Crumbling all over the dreams
Left behind
For a much slower curtain call
The roll and squelch of mud
Between gnarled toes
Towed away
To make way for regrets
And flooded fields
Drenched in oceans of wine
And vomit rising
To drown out the voices

Of lava-laid corpses
Melting in that same twilight
That same echo
Softer now
Finding room for each fading whisper
In a damaged ear

I cannot find my way
In such darkness
I think I'll just sit and wait
For death
To persuade me otherwise
To rip away my memories
And fly away with them
Leaving a smug cadaver
And a final sly wink
At all that could have been
But was never meant to be

www.ingramcontent.com/pod-product-compliance
Lightning Source LLC
Chambersburg PA
CBHW070920080526
44589CB00013B/1383